Chapter 1

Pegasus

Long ago in Greece, there lived a handsome prince named Bellerophon*. He was strong, brave, and loved by everyone... except the king.

3

* say bel-**lair**-o-fon

The king wanted to get rid of Bellerophon. So, he thought up a plan and sent for the prince.

"Think you're brave, do you?" he sneered. "We'll soon see about that."

You must kill the Chimera*, a terrible beast that keeps eating my people.

4

Eager to obey his king, Bellerophon set off to find the monster. On the way, an old lady stopped him.

"First, you must catch the winged horse, Pegasus," she said.

"Find Pegasus and you will be safe from the beast. Pegasus is strong and swift and flies like a bird."

5

After searching for days,
Bellerophon found the horse
high up in the mountains.

"What a beauty," he gasped.

Pegasus was wild and free,
with powerful beating wings.
Catching him wouldn't be easy.

In a flash of silvery light,
the goddess Athene* appeared.
She held out a golden bridle
to Bellerophon.

This is a
magic bridle. It
will help you catch
Pegasus.

"If you put this over the horse's
head, Pegasus will become
tame," she said.

7

Bellerophon thanked Athene and hid behind a rock near a river. When Pegasus came to drink, Bellerophon tiptoed out.

Very quietly, he crept up to Pegasus and slipped the bridle over the horse's head.

Startled, Pegasus reared up. "Steady," said Bellerophon. The horse calmed down and Bellerophon climbed onto his back.

Spreading his wings, Pegasus soared into the sky.

As they flew on, the air grew hot, steamy and smelly.

"Ugh!" said the prince as he sniffed. "That's disgusting! We must be near the Chimera."

They flew down in time to see the beast leaving its cave.

The Chimera didn't have just one head. It had two: a goat-head, with terrible horns, and a  lion-head which breathed fire.

Even its tail was an evil-  looking snake. It spat at Bellerophon, trying to sting him with poison.

Pegasus flew closer and the prince fired his arrows. The lion roared. Huge flames shot from its mouth.

Pegasus rose above the fire
and Bellerophon shot more
arrows. They struck the goat-
head and the snake-tail.

Then the prince took out his
spear and stuck a lump of lead
on the end of it.

The mouth of the lion-head
opened wide to roar and
Bellerophon plunged his spear
down the lion-head's throat.

As the lead melted, the
lion-head gave a howl of pain
and the beast collapsed. The
Chimera was dead.

Bellerophon went back to the king and told him the good news.

I've killed the Chimera, your majesty!

The king wasn't too pleased, but his people were delighted.

"Bellerophon's a hero," they cried. "He's like a god!"

All this praise made
Bellerophon big-headed.

"Maybe I am a god," he said. "If I beat the Chimera, I must be!" So he flew to Mount Olympus, where the gods lived.

Time to go home.

Zeus, the king of the gods, was annoyed to see the prince and sent a bee to sting Pegasus. The horse reared up, throwing Bellerophon off.

Bellerophon fell through the clouds to the ground and was killed in an instant.

Then Zeus caught Pegasus and rode him home to Mount Olympus.

Faster, Pegasus, faster!

From that day on, Pegasus lived with the gods, pulling Zeus across the sky in a chariot made of gold.

Chapter 2

The greedy griffin

Hassan was a farmer, but the only animals on his farm were his two beloved oxen.

One day, he was working in the fields when, suddenly, the sky went dark.

Hassan looked up. Was it about to rain? But he didn't see a cloud overhead...

...he saw a griffin! A griffin was a terrifying creature. It had the head and wings of an eagle, but the body of a lion.

Swooping down, the griffin
snatched up the two oxen in
its lion's claws.

Hassan ran away in terror.
With a few flaps of its giant
wings, the griffin was gone.

Back at home, Hassan sat down and wept.

"There is no hope," he sobbed. "The griffin will eat my oxen. I have nothing." His friends tried to cheer him up.

Feeling a little better,
Hassan and his friends set off
to find the griffin. For hours
they climbed, higher and
higher into the mountains.

All at once, Hassan stopped.

Oh no!
The griffin's
eaten him...

Maybe the
other one's
still alive.

Higher up the mountain still, they came across what they thought was a strange plant.

"What a funny tree," said one of the men.

Hassan shook his head. "It's not a tree," he said.

It's a griffin's feather!

Just then, they heard a loud noise. *Ahhhhhhh... uhhhhh.*

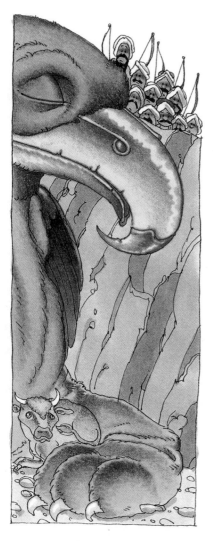

"W-w-w-what's that?" the men whispered, looking over the rocks.

There was the griffin, fast asleep and snoring, with the ox trapped by its paw.

"Quick, before it wakes!"
cried Hassan. As fast as they
could, the men put arrows
to their bows and fired them.

The griffin woke up with
a mighty bellow. But it was
too late.

A hail of arrows struck its
chest. As the griffin fell back,
Hassan's ox jumped up and
ran to safety.

And, from then on, whenever
Hassan worked in his fields, he
checked for strange clouds first.

27

Chapter 3

The evil cockatrice

There was once a farmer
named Zak. He and his wife,
Beela, were happy but very
poor. Their only animals were
a few hens and a rooster.

One day, the rooster began running around and around in circles, while crowing loudly.

"Beela! Come and look at this!" called Zak.

Cock-a-doodle-doo!

The rooster sat down and ruffled its feathers.

"He looks like he's about to lay an egg," said Beela.

"But roosters can't!" said Zak.

They stared. This one *had* laid an egg and it was huge.

A few minutes later, the egg began to crack. A tiny rooster comb appeared.

The rooster stared at the egg with its beady eyes. Suddenly it gave a great squawk and rolled over, dead.

Zak and Beela gasped in horror as a snake crawled out of the egg. It sat up proudly and looked around.

Beela saw its beady red eyes and pointy rooster's comb.

"A cockatrice!" she screamed.

"What's a cockatrice?"
asked Zak.

"It's a very evil creature,"
said Beela. "It's only born
when a rooster lays an egg."

The cockatrice slithered off.
Everything it touched was
burned, leaving a horrible
scorched trail.

Anything that looked into the creature's creepy red eyes died immediately.

"We must warn everyone!" cried Beela. She and Zak ran to the village leader.

The cockatrice is dangerous!

The village leader sent a brave soldier to kill the cockatrice. The soldier wore a helmet to protect his eyes and blindfolded his horse, too.

We'll catch the nasty beast...

"Do be careful!" Beela called out, as he left.

The soldier rode along,
looking for the cockatrice.

When he
found a
scorched
field, he
knew it was
near. Then
he saw it.

Charging
up, he raised
his spear and
stabbed the
cockatrice as
hard as he
could.

As the spear went in, the
soldier shouted out in pain. It
was as though poison had shot
up the spear into his arm.

My arm! It's
burning!

He fell from his horse and
lay still, unable to move. The
cockatrice wasn't hurt at all.

The villagers were terrified that the cockatrice would kill them all.

"Perhaps the old priest can help," said Zak.

Let's see...
You'll need a mirror.

"To kill the creature, you must show it a reflection of itself," the priest said.

Zak and Beela ran off to fetch the biggest mirror they could find. Then they hid behind some rocks, to wait.

When the cockatrice arrived, they crept forward, holding the mirror in front of them.

As soon as the cockatrice saw itself, it let out a desperate shriek.

Zak and Beela peeked around the mirror. The cockatrice was dead on the ground. Its evil eyes had claimed their last victim.

Chapter 4

Unicorn magic

Once, there was a king who believed unicorn horns were magic. "Find me a unicorn!" he cried to Toby, his page. "And don't come home without one."

Toby hunted all over the world, but he couldn't find a unicorn anywhere.

Days became weeks...
weeks became months...
months became years...

Contents

Stories of Magical Animals

Retold by
Carol Watson

Adapted by Gill Harvey

Illustrated by Nick Price

Reading Consultant: Alison Kelly
University of Surrey Roehampton